The Book of Motion

The Book of Motion

POEMS BY TUNG-HUI HU

The University of Georgia Press   Athens and London

Published by the University of Georgia Press
Athens, Georgia 30602
© 2003 by Tung-Hui Hu
All rights reserved
Designed by Mindy Basinger Hill
Set in 10.5/15 Minion
Printed and bound by McNaughton & Gunn, Inc.
The paper in this book meets the guidelines for
permanence and durability of the Committee on
Production Guidelines for Book Longevity of the
Council on Library Resources.

Printed in the United States of America
07   06   05   04   03   P   5   4   3   2   1

Library of Congress Cataloging-in-Publication Data

Hu, Tung-Hui, 1974–
The book of motion : poems / by Tung-Hui Hu.
p. cm. — (The contemporary poetry series)
ISBN 0-8203-2568-6 (pbk. : alk. paper)
I. Title. II. Series: Contemporary poetry series
(University of Georgia Press)
PS3608.U22 B66 2003
811'.6—dc21
2003008367

British Library Cataloging-in-Publication Data available

Contents

—

The Book of Motion

Some arrivals

A rock a fish

Here there is breath.
There are rocks, but only
as an abdomen pulled
apart, that red color of
correction marks, cracked
lips, and swellings.
The people who live here,
stringy men, wispy
women, as if spun from
clouds, they are capable
of greater passions than
us: one man, infuriated
at his car, the lemon
that had cost him a life's
savings, drove it to the
canyon edge and cut away
the metal cord that coupled
the car, the rocks. Sliding
through the waters,
it breathed, and its gills
began to whiten with air—
how small the car must
have looked from above,
but to the fish it was as if
a continent had shifted,
stretched, and birthed
a new mountain range.

The chess match

Every move involves an abuse of power,
said the general to his opponent
with a friendly wave. The brilliant strategist
could do nothing more but nod as he thought of
long summer nights spent in European bars,
languidly, as if the world had become
a gigantic swamp
with fluid ground and the sound of cicadas
the wind blowing just enough
to catch his hair, now marsh-grass
and the waitress's face was flushed, too,
as she set a drink before him
and turned with slender legs into a heron.
Every move involves an abuse of power,
but by now the only things that moved
lived in his head
(was the night starry or overcast?
do cicadas actually live in swamps?)
and he set the general's words aside
and began to play.

The siege

The catapult fired rocks every minute,
on the minute, each beat constant
and steady as a radio report until
it is derailed by a news flash:
all the land under siege by snow,
expected to lift in March,
nowhere for the sheep to graze,
they'll have to stay in the living
room, we've whole pastures of
cloth couches there, the town
will burn down if the snow
doesn't get to it first, but at least
we have enough rocks to build
another castle, next time we'll
just welcome the attackers inside
and serenade them with '*O sole mio*
sung off-key until they grow
weary of war.

Story told to yourself

It is early spring my stomach
is hurting there is a pool at
midnight and several cherry
trees around it the air is still
cold do the blossoms break when
touched or could I save any?
was noch wacht auf mitten

im Februar tut es der Erde weh?
what else awakes now does
the earth hurt? the trees are
quiet and muscular and im halbes
Licht finde ich die Bäume so
nah wie Beine von der Erde
as legs from the soil I can't

find my way out of the place
any more understand how
I hated this city stolen from
a swamp where the streets
shrink away from your touch?
how easily I lost the city of my
childhood saving only the
cherry trees beside the pond I
remember the year

after I left there were miles
of dead fish in the pool:
winter came early that year
and raised out of the waters
a white never meant to be
found by you or me.

Poem in memory of a house

1. THE OCCUPATION
   Homes were going up all over the hillside.
   You'd turn your back for a second
   and pop! up went a new house.
   Endless columns of wood like a scene
   of the crucifixion. Real estate agents
   armed with walkie-talkies barking at
   half-finished meadows, driveways
   wet and congealing. Nothing could
   stop them. They had the noble
   look of Xerxes lashing the sea.

2. THE THEFT
   Needing parts for a tree house
   I stole door frames.
   Wood parts were lying
   in heaps of sawdust
   like organs in an operating room
   still fresh and uncorrupted.
   Wooden limbs and splinters.
   In dreams that night
   my conscience chased me
   through hill and dale.
   My whole kingdom for
   a door frame, it said.
   It was a bad time for the
   land. The surgeons had
   termites in their legs.

3. A HALF YEAR LATER

We are creating an open society
where anyone who wants an
education can get an education
and anyone who wants to be
embarrassed can be embarrassed
without fear of reprisal.
Our society will be a house without
walls where you can see clear
to the ends of the earth
and when it rains it rains
and when you feel the sun rising
on your skin and you discover
you are only in your underwear
you will have forgotten what
it means to be ashamed.

4. THE HONEYMOON

But you wouldn't actually live
in one of these houses, maybe
squat inside the basement until
you are evicted, or egg one on
Halloween as an afterthought,
but it was always something
abstract and unlivable: purgatory,
for instance. Even when you
had summoned up the courage
to unlock the door you were still
trespassing. Discovering your
name on the mailbox came
with a feeling of guilt
like sharing the last name
of a famous murderer.

Vigilance

After the cold
there was a long safe period which I will
describe as "1996 vintage with oak flavors."
Nothing could compare. Even the most
vigilant of museum guards deface paintings
from time to time, but
how safe I felt! I could have
leaped off roofs and someone would have caught me
and handed me a nice glass of warm milk afterward.
Safety in numbers, they said,
and there were so many of us that
if one died the others would close in after him
effortlessly like water.
Some bankers offered us a briefcase full of gold
if we would tell them how to feel so safe
while facing the demons of existence.
Which demons? I asked, but only
out of politeness. They were always
exaggerating when they talked to me,
saying gold and meaning office supplies.

The tree of conscience

Some people walk past and complain of being stared at. "Do your laundry!" it shouts after them. Or, "Sin more!" Others fall asleep under it, knowing the eyes will watch over them. Sometimes the wind, which has no conscience, will come over and tap the tree lightly— then the eyes close, and knotholes appear in its place.

Maximum occupancy 38 persons

Without the erosion of conversation,
there is only a faint scent of
footsteps, a trail of suede
splinters toward the door.

Entranced by the afternoon sun,
two carved blocks of ice dissolve
into each other, forming a clear
soup we might mistake for love.

Without the erosion of conversation,
dust settles over floor wounds,
a second skin. A passing bird pauses
for the look inside but cannot see
the ladle dangling lewdly over
the punch bowl or the clock's hands
saluting sunrise, sunset, and
sunrise again.

Love poem to Moira

The girl who looks like she's always about to weep, sitting in the corner. It was hard to grow up in her shadows! One moment we'll be talking about porcupines, the next second she's perched atop a piano. The last time I felt so happy was when I wrestled with the Old Man of the Sea, ages ago, long before I met you. By way of explanation she says: "I always laugh while I'm kissing someone." Moira, why didn't you tell me earlier? We could spend endless hours in the dark room upstairs writing each other poems, or if you'd like, crying ourselves to sleep.

Migrations at night

1. A dark forest with barely
   any light. Overhead the only
   source of comprehension
   illuminates several ink stains
   on trees sliced paper-thin.

2. The tides the lunacies
   the clearer light are
   all explanations for the
   phenomenon that causes
   many men to wake up
   the next day with teeth
   marks on their bodies.

3. Meeting someone for
   three hours in a garden
   telephone poles over you
   fatherly and chapped
   all the sounds of paradise
   as the gate closes: you would
   howl at the moon but
   now you are so young that
   your voice would crack.

4. But it was so dark outside
   that he entered the wrong
   house and, to his delight,
   woke up in the wrong arms.

5. The stars were getting dimmer.
   One time we worried the sky
   would fade away altogether.
   Birds kept losing their way
   and would tumble out
   of the sky in a hail of wings,
   beaks, scrolls, until finally they
   stopped daring each other
   to close their eyes at night.

Early morning in Denver

The time when everything was
the same but had different names.
It's early morning and I'm waking
up in an airplane and land masses
outside with many outlines,

undifferentiated, bluish-gray shadows.
The world has not yet been built,
it can still float away, the lines are weak
as the legs of a newborn animal.
And I find myself inside that infinite

cornfield, bluish-yellow light from
sunrise, a tornado on the horizon.
Stalks bending away from the plane
which has fallen from the invisible
and into Denver. (A city like

any other city.) Rocks turn
in the breeze, a hollow,
statues of coal, light rising out of
light like mountains: over the humped
back of turtles, ancient beasts. Even

the tortoise who once held up
the world on his shell is soil now, or mud.

Red wine: An advertisement

"When I wake up I am
so innocent you can
remind me of murders
& I will say yes,
it was a silly game I
played when young,
what did you do?
But the day is cruel
& by noontime I have
begun to talk back to
people, my boss &
the president on TV
yes even the neighbor's
rottweiler. I talk to
many important people
though there is no time
to remember them all
& when I go home I am
about ready to burst.
Only at night after a
glass of red wine do I see
people as they really are
& when I sleep
I look like a child again,"
he said, (firmly)
into the microphone.

Welcome back

The wrong man came through the door,
Asked for a glass of water. For my headache,
He said. We passed him a tumbler
And waited for him to unpack
His travel stories, the pale Riesling wine,
A wood chess set, a ticket stub with
Her phone number, or maybe the plan was
She bursting out of his head,
Thereby evading immigration officers.

But he didn't move, just drank
Like a summer plant,
While the sky slowly expired
To the tune of cars parking.
He was breathing heavily,
And we could feel it curling toward
Champagne bottles already sweating
So we asked him to leave. There wasn't
Enough light left to go around.

Some arrivals

It was warmer today,
and the pavement was cracked open
like an old person's skin,

sunburned and pale,
mosaic weathered,
a balding head.

The alarm clock rang
for hours in ecstasy,
and people broke bones

unused for months
as they awoke again,
their wrinkled hands

lined with old injuries,
private and unspeakable
as a season changing.

Elegies for self

They found me lying in the fountain. It had rained and I was floating next to magnolia leaves. Pennies had slid off the mouths of carved stone fish and they were glad to talk of more than money. From time to time a child waded in and splashed wantonly until the scent of magnolias would circle upward refreshed by the change of pace.

How long had I been there? One time the fountain froze over and the water slowed to the point that water striders awoke statuesque to find their limbs immobilized. One tore its leg off. I, too, awoke, but as a sleepwalker does, intent on moving, yet infirm in spirit. Thoughts faint as an insect trapped in amber.

They are medicating me and watching how I sleep. They are worried I will roll off the mattress and I dream about an intern who waits at the foot of the bed, palms extended, to catch my falling body. They turn off the lights and there are still pools of blackness around the room that are difficult to erase. I think I can see my veins: crystalline, red as clay. Even the valves in my heart remind me of pottery.

A janitor, who is so old that her skin is transparent, has the job of keeping my room clear. She mops the floor so thoroughly she says it is clean enough to eat on. She sweeps everywhere but the ceiling, and I worry that any escape I make will be dust ridden, that I will become dirt in a spider web.

To escape the heat I hid inside the chapel. The air was cool as I pressed myself against the stone floor. I heard the footsteps of rats and angels, the movements of stained glass. A philosopher was stooping under the weight of his halo and despite the moonlight his aura began turning a coarse, thick color. Other windows watched but would not break the arthritic silence.

I saw many strange things until the morning, when the sun broke and glazed the eyes of the saints into place. The air was narcotic as summer. You could hear a bird singing out the window, or a truck backing up.

They were kicking bottles through the park: savagely, like they meant it. They were splintering into fourths, fifths, and you could see the rings of glass split open until it was a burial ground, strewn with flower heads.

It was autumn: even the pebbles were turning colors, green and brown.

It was an oceanic time for all of us. There were endless shoals of linoleum outside my office and once while en route to the bathroom I ran aground and broke my ankle. "Better watch where you're going," the watchman said.

The corridors were coiled up like serpents. "If you step on them, they bite back," they warned us. They found one man cradled vicelike between the walls, but left him there, unable to pull him loose.

The floors were endless and seemed to reach all the way to the Pacific. We spent lunch hours talking about what was at the horizon. One worker claimed he had been there, and seen a city outside, dry and lifeless as bone. Simply breathing the air would turn your lungs to dust.

I was the best sleeper in the class, and one time it seemed like I would never wake up. The whole class crowded around while the teacher stood forlornly at the head of the room and rapped out the time with a ruler. How long I had practiced for this momentous event! First by lowering myself slowly into the pond and waking to waters endless as insomnia, the liquid press of the eyelids; then by going to airports and meditating until my heart rate matched the tempo of planes taking off. Seals, too, lower their pulse when preparing to dive into the abyss, but often are so enraptured by the depths that they forget to return to normal speed. It is as if everyone has decided to become salesmen. In the same way I knew the class was chattering, bored by such feats of virtue. Already one boy was scribbling on his desk, and the teacher had started the next lesson.

The buildings were swaying to the point of collapse and they had to block the street off for several weeks. The dust was so great it left you with a terrible paleness that tasted like aspirin. The citizens shuffled past the metal dividers and never mentioned the block in conversation, as if it no longer existed.

In that time children came out and scrambled over the plaster cairns. Their eyes were bleached white and their hair was graying. These were the oldest children in the world.

Pompeii still moved. From afar the street seemed a gift package, wrapped in yellow CAUTION tape, something that would be delivered to the city pure and whole again.

after Aris Alexandrou

Later we walked outside and my feet had become cobblestones, filling to the brim with dirt. The rain fell over us and I watched a November afternoon wash away, distant and useless as a storm on television.

My teeth were chattering. I pictured the sunflowers in the meadows with necks snapping from watching the sun too long. Miles grew between us. I watched blackbirds take off and found that they were my fingers waving good-bye.

That year the city ground to a halt and the stars rarely came out at night. Wild dogs roamed the dockyards and alleyways, growing bony with idleness, no longer hunting anything. One prisoner escaped because the guards were too tired to catch him. I watched him run down the valley, arms stretched outward, his silhouette against the horizon: he was the first constellation we had seen in years.

Last night a stranger walked past me on the way home. She smiled sadly when I looked away, and waved her arms, which were long and stemmed under the moonlight.

Today I spread a newspaper over the wet field and sat down, waiting. Damp headlines asking me what I wanted in life. I saw a thousand *I*s in the articles, scattered between the blades of grass like stars. O multiplicity of selves, one of me is running away from home, another safely stowed away below deck, a third playing Chopin to a salesman. When she arrived, as I imagine she did, I tried to get up, but it was like the first step on land, having been at sea all your life.

Startled by thunder, I tumbled down the hill and tore my pants badly. I stuck my hands through a flap of cloth to see if I was all right. To my surprise it was your knee that I felt. As soon as I got home I took my clothes off in front of the mirror and was overwhelmed by the abundance of bones—some which I had never noticed before in my life, like the ulna and the radius, some looking like they had been dragged out of the darkness for the first time—and above all, your knee, beautiful as the first day I laid eyes upon it, perhaps a bit out of place, looking as if it would kick back if touched the wrong way. And you (who I knew only as a jumble of body parts, who appeared in dreams always incomplete, as hands or lips carved from stone), will you forgive me for this act of indiscretion, this mix-up?

They sent me across the country with a blank letter of introduction. Hundreds of miles I traveled on trains and stopped in nameless towns to show them the photograph album, which was worn and had the wary look of foreignness woven into its spine. Most people ignored me or indulged me until I bought their vacant, bone-rimmed cups of coffee—then they turned to go. But some watched with a wistful look on their faces as I showed them pictures of cities, those paeans of concrete and glass, where thousands of people could gather in a park, and none of them with exactly the same face. They shared a nostalgia for endings, and when I pulled out my letter of introduction, they said no need. I would be shown a room, and there I would stay until my welcome had worn out.

Fast lives

Hill climbing

Like bruised hearts, he said, that's what wild strawberries look like.
But they had broken so many you could hear a pair of lovers
    weeping beneath the field.

Above them the sky was green copper. A swollen taste from the rain.
With provocation it would echo back three heartbeats in a row, in a
    coincidence.

The ascent uphill was rough.
It was amazing how long they could last on one pulse of breath: he
    talked to himself mostly, her hair looked like hell, their shoes
    were stained red.
Then it was over. The view was nothing special. You'd make a lousy
    Indian, she said.

Overreactions & other professions of faith

I swallowed some habaneros to
see what it was like to breathe fire.
The pain grew in the stomach
like money, I suppose, grows
on trees. Having had neither pain
nor money in my life the
experience was out of this world.
I could have swallowed the Nile
if they paid for the plane ticket.
Fire hugged me from inside until
I could burst, and I did, yelling
obscenities from mountaintops to
passing tourists, who thought I
might be overreacting a bit. Drink
some milk, they said, as if milk
would be enough to curdle my
emotions. A priest wanted to take
my picture. He had never seen
anyone so passionate about life, so
endangered. Would he cut me open
to discover a dead youth inside?

Fragile

Midnights we walked in mountains they broke off pieces of ankle
      pieces of toe bones
we reached in the water and tugged and the tail of a fish pulled out
midnights we stumbled in the dark the hearing of hands and
      fumbles of skin
they slid off and a thousand islands and cliffs arose over the water
midnights we stretched tendons into rivers we washed our names
      into rivers
and unbirthed lost them as easily as the tearing of dragonfly wings
midnights we touched fingertips to rock we poured holes into caves
      into limestone
until wide-eyed you arose and remarked how fragile mornings are
      The breakage of sunlight.

Impossible luxuries

A desert island to yourself,
an ocean bluer than the skies.
Even the sharks are too humble to approach.
A gigantic banquet set on the sand,
thousands of animals have died for
this pleasure, and you aren't hungry.
You are reenacting your first kiss
with the taste of quinine in your mouth.
The woman tells you to finish your plate:
you are happy beyond words,
you don't have anything with which
to compare this happiness,
just the faint memory of the time
when, as a child, you realized
you were going to die someday,
and by inversion,
you were relieved you were still alive.

Pseudoephedrine

I'm not sick, I can't be sick, but here I am,
flat on my back, meek, tranquilized,
elephantine but still very healthy.
Everything moves slowly.
The girl next door has taken several months
to pick up her mail. Lichen, ferns, and small vines
are growing everywhere, turning the walls green,
grinding the floors into loam. Similarly,
everything in the refrigerator has gone bad,
but I can't taste things anymore.
Vegetable cardboard, leftover
cardboard, a world of blank surfaces. Most made
of plaster, some from butcher paper.
I feel a bit drowsy.
All the people who are visiting me
shuffle invisibly through the room, as if at a wake
for a famous person. The one in my corner whispers
to another: "He was once the president of a major country."
They're about to scatter my ashes over the ocean,
and I barely have the chance to object. Look,
my hands are floating miles away, and I have become
massive as a volcano.

Growing up

He said he'd turn over a new leaf on Monday. Eating candy wasn't fun anymore. Also on his list was: being nice to people, and never saying sorry. The other kids laughed at him, but Mom was encouraging, and made a pitcher of cloudy lemonade to celebrate.

On the last day of his childhood, his life flashed before him. It was a momentary feeling at the back of his neck, burning like a mosquito bite, soft as a death of hunger.

Then he grew up. He stopped eating sweets and started to do bad things, like indulge in women. The teacher said he was precocious. He had his first cigarette in the bathroom. The lemonade was left out on the porch and turned swampy with insects.

Fast lives

Next to the ocean,
things live fast,
the bedsheets mildew
after a few days,
your lamps redden
with rust, you try to cut
a piece of bread &
the knife breaks in two,
the wooden balcony
grows tender & worm eaten
as fruit fallen from trees
& when you want a view
the windows are blurry,
quick to temper,
vertiginous windows,
like eyes going blind are
portals to the soul
& nothing more.

Killing flies

That summer there were millions of them festering in the living room. We tried using the atomizer, which we nicknamed the disintegrator, but the challenge wasn't there. So we'd lure them off one by one and thwack them on the side of the heads and they were so dumb they didn't do anything except keep sacrificing themselves as the hours went past and the sun lost its balance and rolled down the hill. Hasta la vista, baby! as I climbed onto the piano to perform the last rites atop a stack of Schumann's *Kinderlieder* and then out went the rubber band and then like a firing squad—out went the lights. Some flies made the front page of the *New York Times*. Everyone was having too much fun. Only once did we miss and that was to see how they would react. Would it warn the others? Would it die of gratitude?

The oracle grants a rare interview

When they look me up in the yearbook
I imagine them saying

a few years ago his mind began to fail
like an overloaded dryer,
the words out of his mouth
froth and no substance
a far cry from the years when
we knew him:

someone who loved people
with the patience
of oceans and traffic cops,
he was the field where
Midas confessed his sins,

after school let out
he would lie senseless
and watch the skies,
which were empty,
beautiful as eggshells.

Dry

She had a hard time concentrating the month she quit drinking. The driest things she could think of were fault lines in the desert, and it was only a matter of time before she decided on a vacation to Phoenix. On the long plane ride over, she closed her eyes and prepared herself for the month-long drought. She fancied herself a phoenix carved into the desert. The fires would enter her ribs and consume her like a ticklish lover, and then at the climax she would throw off her ash-colored robe and run barefoot into the sunset. She would sow dirt from her hands the way Johnny Appleseed dealt out springtime; she would frown until the wrinkles on her forehead were canyons, ancient marks of wisdom. The only thing that worried her was rainfall. It was something that would blur her away, leaving her huddled indoors in the hotel lobby, sipping gutter water from a champagne glass.

You were born to live on an island

That summer it had reached
the melting point. Mornings
the skin ached like bark
blown off a tree. I saw a squirrel
half immersed in dirt,
breathing only enough
not to drown, fur knotted
as if a rug: it was this easy
to move between life and
not-life, solid and liquid.
Oranges shriveled down to
nothing and your back
turned into a small desert.
At night we felt sandstorms
tear through our bodies.

The shore

A clerk, who has lost his
night vision from being
inside too long, goes out
to piss under the August
stars and does not notice
the thousands of motorists
looking at him with wonder.
Walking alongside the road
he keeps running into things
in the dark, things that have
washed up on the shoreline:
gas cans, bones. Thousands
of cars swim backward,
forward, wishing they could
stop as easily. Each time he
opens his eyes he sees
the innards of a whale,
its ribcage of street lamps
arched over the freeway.
Asphalt veins. No water—
the summer is drying up,
like a clot.

Snow over the cornfields

I don't mean to exaggerate.
Snow over the cornfields is not something
I'd normally write you about
but I think I've found
the place where people go after they die.

You know the mosaic pattern you see
when you are flying over the countryside?
Well, it snowed just lightly enough
that it looked like the skin of a man
newly arisen from the ocean,
white with brine,

white and brown,
the patterns were exactly this:
tattoos on his skin, tattoos of
eagle feathers and jackals and lizards,
all in pieces, in squares,

also, men hunched into squares,
necks bent & legs twisted,
the same thing as Aztec carvings on stone,

but cut into the earth, into the fields.
Can you imagine?

That's what I was thinking of as I flew
over Nebraska. Feathers chiseled into your body.

The mapmaker

The city was full of joyriders who went
from stop to stop leaving a trail of crumbs
that pigeons ate as a matter of principle.
The bus drivers were prone to bribery
and refused to take passengers who knew
where they were going. Tourists shopped
compulsively in the hopes of meeting a
beautiful stranger who would fall in love
at first sight and give them directions.
In truth only the mapmaker understood
why the river vanished after sunset and
why the streets curved into each other
like interlocking crescents of hair.
The mapmaker's tower was filled with
crystal telescopes that never moved and
maps perfect and unreadable as palm lines,
maps so addictive that the city would grind
to a halt for days if he made a mistake.
Airplane pilots pored over the maps
looking for a place to land: the clever
ones used highways or secluded grottoes.
To pass the time, the passengers told each
other stories of cities so primitive that
the citizens still took the same route to
work each day, who dreamt of geometries
and were haunted by their past.

What happens next

Summers we used to go down to Atlantic City and tell people their fortunes. Under the shade of lemon trees a bunch of us would set up camp and wave passersby over, and come they did, at first to escape the sun, but soon a flock, each with flushed faces and quivering mouths. What did they want from us, what were they like? Well, an old woman wanted to know if she would give birth: her face was thick and scarred, the drawings of a child playing with markers, but bold, like tire marks. We took many breaks as the spirits did not speak to us constantly but grew tired of our stream of questions. What a pleasant time, sitting on the beach and deciding what happens next. Does the girl get sacrificed after all, or will she escape to the Aegean in time? Does the mother kill the father when he gets home, or does she go back to the kitchen? We read so many palms that sometimes we got them confused. Every so often someone would go back home and marry the wrong person. After that we were quiet as starlings in a cage.

Notes

"Maximum occupancy 38 persons" was first published in *Many Mountains Moving*. "Poem in memory of a house" first appeared in *AGNI Online* (June 2003). The title "You were born to live on an island" is from Octavio Paz's "Naciste para vivir en una isla" in *Madrigal*. "Story told to yourself" is after James Laughlin's *In Another Country*. "Pseudoephedrine" refers to pseudoephedrine sulfate and pseudoephedrine hydrochloride, which are active ingredients in many over-the-counter decongestants and are mild vasoconstrictors. The line "does she go back to the kitchen" (in "What happens next") is after Christa Wolf's question about Clytemnestra, "Was she to . . . go cringing back to the hearth and the distaff?"

I am indebted to Laurie Sheck for her counsel and wisdom. I would also like to thank my family, friends, and the staff at the University of Georgia Press.

THE CONTEMPORARY POETRY SERIES
EDITED BY PAUL ZIMMER